ULTIMATE COMICS SPIDER-MAN

WRITER: **BRIAN MICHAEL BENDIS**

ARTIST, #16.1: **DAVID MARQUEZ**

ARTIST, #19-22: **SARA PICHELLI**

COLOR ARTIST: **JUSTIN PONSOR**

LETTERER: **VC'S CORY PETIT**

COVER ART: **DAVID MARQUEZ** & **JUSTIN PONSOR** (#16.1), **SARA PICHELLI** & **RAINIER BEREDO** (#19 & #21-22) AND **SARA PICHELLI** & **CHRISTINA STRAIN** (#20)

ASSISTANT EDITORS: **EMILY SHAW** & **JON MOISAN**

EDITOR: **MARK PANICCIA**

COLLECTION EDITOR: **JENNIFER GRÜNWALD**

ASSOCIATE MANAGING EDITOR: **ALEX STARBUCK**

EDITOR, SPECIAL PROJECTS: **MARK D. BEAZLEY**

SENIOR EDITOR, SPECIAL PROJECTS: **JEFF YOUNGQUIST**

SVP PRINT, SALES & MARKETING: **DAVID GABRIEL**

EDITOR IN CHIEF: **AXEL ALONSO**

CHIEF CREATIVE OFFICER: **JOE QUESADA**

PUBLISHER: **DAN BUCKLEY**

EXECUTIVE PRODUCER: **ALAN FINE**

PREVIOUSLY:

MILES FOUND OUT THAT HIS FATHER AND HIS UNCLE AARON USED TO BE CRIMINALS. HIS DAD REFORMED BUT HIS UNCLE BECAME A WORLD-CLASS CRIMINAL KNOWN AS THE PROWLER. UNCLE AARON CONFRONTED MILES WITH THE TRUTH AND CONVINCED MILES TO JOIN HIM IN TAKING DOWN A REAL SUPER VILLAIN...THE SCORPION.

MILES REALIZED THAT HIS UNCLE WAS USING HIM, AND THEY HAD A CONFRONTATION THAT TURNED VIOLENT. UNCLE AARON DIED WHEN HIS BATTLESUIT BACKFIRED. THIS ALL HAPPENED IN FRONT OF A CROWD.

DURING THE BOLD ATTACKS OF A GRASSROOTS TERRORIST MILITIA KNOWN AS HYDRA THAT HAD DECLARED WAR ON THE STATUS QUO, MILES'S FATHER WAS TAKEN INTO S.H.I.E.L.D. CUSTODY ONLY TO BE RESCUED BY HYDRA. THEY HANDED HIM A GUN AND ASKED HIM TO JOIN THEIR REVOLUTION. HE, IN TURN, ATTACKED THEM AND RAN AWAY.

SPIDER-MAN BY BRIAN MICHAEL BENDIS VOL. 4. Contains material originally published in magazine form as ULTIMATE COMICS SPIDER-MAN #16.1 and #19-22. First printing 2014. ISBN#). Published by MARVEL WORLDWIDE, INC., a subsidiary of MARVEL ENTERTAINMENT, LLC. OFFICE OF PUBLICATION: 135 West 50th Street, New York, NY 10020. **Printed** FINE, EVP - Office of the President, Marvel Worldwide, Inc. and EVP & CMO Marvel Characters B.V.; DAN BUCKLEY, Publisher & President - Print, Animation & Digital Divisions; JOE QUESADA, r; TOM BREVOORT, SVP of Publishing; DAVID BOGART, SVP of Operations & Procurement, Publishing; C.B. CEBULSKI, SVP of Creator & Content Development; DAVID GABRIEL, SVP Print, Sales & EFE, VP of Operations & Logistics; DAN CARR, Executive Director of Publishing Technology; SUSAN CRESPI, Editorial Operations Manager; ALEX MORALES, Publishing Operations Manager; STAN itus. For information regarding advertising in Marvel Comics or on Marvel.com, please contact Niza Disla, Director of Marvel Partnerships, at ndisla@marvel.com. For Marvel subscription inquiries, -9158. **Manufactured between 1/24/2014 and 3/3/2014 by R.R. DONNELLEY, INC., SALEM, VA, USA.**

16.1

POINT•ONE

BROADWAY

DAILY BUGLE

NEW SPIDER-MAN
A DANGER

DAILY BUGLE

FLLWOOM

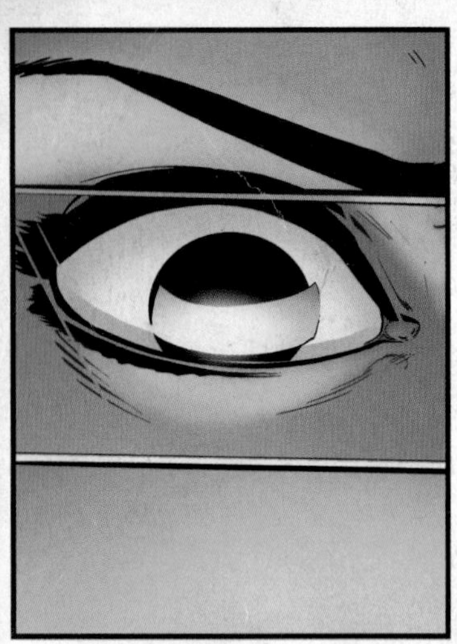

Oh my God!

You are...
just...
...like me.

What?
What did you say?

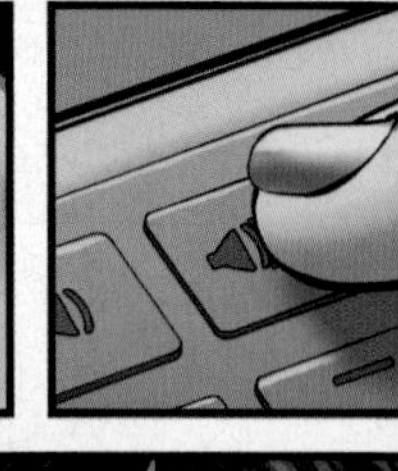

They're calling someone.
Hold on.
You are...
just...
...like me.

Do you see this?
Is that the new Spider-Man?

Jeez...

Dear lord!
Someone call 9-1-1!
That was crazy.
How about...
...that?

You are...
just...
...like me.

You are...
just...
...like me.

Daily Bugle, Midtown Manhattan

According to my sources, Stark Enterprises will profit from this latest war to the tune of $19 billion.
So you're saying Stark started a war to make some money?
No. I'm saying that Stark Enterprises is about to make a profit of $19 billion.
I think that deserves further investigation.
Next.
The New York Times ran a poll that said that 46% of the country ***still*** doesn't believe that the person who is saying he is Captain America is the ***original*** Captain America.
A propaganda tool.
Who do they ***think*** he is?
Of who?

I'm not running that.
Does anybody have anything that even slightly resembles an interesting take on an interesting story?
This country almost collapsed in civil war and none of you have anything interesting to write about?

I have something on this new Spider-Man.

Is it good?

This is amateur footage of the fight between Spider-Man and who the F.B.I. called The Prowler.
Now The Prowler's real name is--was Aaron Davis.
He was a cat burglar of some report, hence the name.
Before that just low-level, all-around scum his entire life.

But what's interesting is how crazy he got just about the same time this new Spider-Man popped up in our lives.
He started wearing gear and challenging the big dogs.
He's reportedly the one who took out *The Scorpion*.

That's true.
Spider-Man was there.
That's my point.

There is *some connection* between The Prowler and this new Spider-Man.
It looks like they were partnered up and then things went sour.
And if you can--well you can't hear but just before he dies...
He says something like:
You are...
just...
...like me.

And?

And if you look, see, you can see the new Spider-Man, he might be African-American.

What does *that* mean?

I think they might be related.
All my life.
How long have you lived in New York, Miss Brant?
And am I the first person to tell you that not all African-American people are related?

Thank you for that, Robbie.
But no.
There's a familiarity here. Between these two.
I think they *knew* each oth
very well.
I think they might related.

I don't know.
I just think the country almost cracked itself in half under the foot of civil war.
I think there are bigger things to write about.
Well good for me that you aren't the editor-in-chief of this newspaper, Urich.
You're just a reporter like me and I don't have to ask *you* what I should be writing about.

Whatever you are looking for, you don't have it yet.
Don't come back into this room with nothing.
Don't come at me with something I can see on YouTube.
45 minutes till we lock the late edition.
GO!!

Are we really looking to out the new Spider-Man?

What is the story *about?*

A master criminal has a connection of some sort to this new Spider-Man.
We don't know anything about him.
You told me you go poking around and I think there is something here.

So the death of Peter Parker taught us nothing?

I was guarding her!! That's all I was doing!!
Officer Maddox.
Wow. Betty Brant.
You'd better not let my captain see you around here after that thing you wro--
I need a favor.

Wow.
A favor I will gladly return.
You have gigantic caliyoodas.

I'm desperate.
Please, John, I promise I will make it up to you.
You are going to get me fired.

I just need to see The Prowler file.
He's dead.

Then what could the harm possibly be?

Brooklyn, New York.

It was the strangest thing.

One day he's living here and the next day he just isn't.

He packed up in the middle of the night and just disappeared.

Still had 3 weeks left on his rent.

I certainly don't mind money for nothin'.

I'm just sayin' it was the strangest thing.

Usually we have to kick people out for ***not*** paying.
What's the rent?
$2,200 a month.
I'll take it.

Great. I'll go get the paperwork.
Great.
I'll be right back.
Great.

PEELED
TOMATOES
AH!

That is the biggest spider I have ever seen.
And it's not--it's not a tarantula.
Is it?

Gonna vomit.

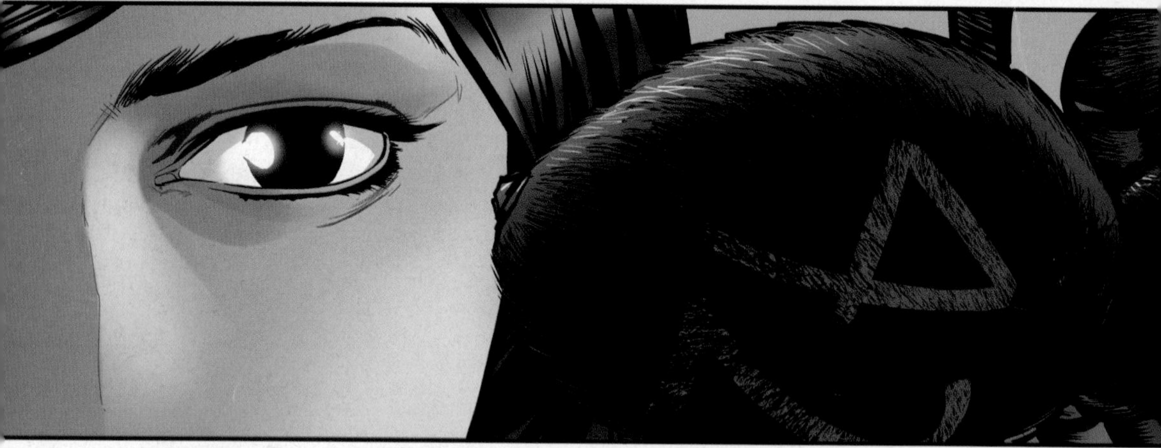

So it's all pretty standard.
We will need first and last months rent plus a couple of--
Uh...

Hello?

Somewhere in New Jersey...
ROXXON
INDUSTRIES

You didn't call me back, Doctor Marcus.
Ah!
You should know me well enough to know not calling me back is not going to make me go away.

Go to hell, Betty.
Seriously, **straight** to hell.
I need your help.
I need **you** to go to hell.
I just need you to--
My interest in what you need after the way you--

What **is** this?
Where did you **get** that?
You **know** what this is.

Where did you **get that??!!**
Let **go** of me!!

Where did you get it??!!
I found it!!
God!!
Was it dead when you found it?
It looks like it's been dead for a long time.

Look at **that.**
It calcified.
You've seen this before?
Yes, I have.

This--this was part of a project I was working on.
You? Here?
No. Oscorp. This was a while ago.

Oscorp?
What does that number mean?

I tell you and my name ends up in another one of your hatchet job rag--
The only way I promise to keep your name out of it is you tell me what it is.
Like I can trust--
I promise!
Do you remember Spider-Man?
The original one?

Well, Peter Parker, it seems, was bit by a spider that was being genetically experimented on at Oscorp.
Once Norman Osborn found out he accidently invented Spider-Man...he spent the rest of his life trying to duplicate that experiment.
He literally killed himself trying to do it.

This was test subject 42.
Where did you find it?

Did it go missing or was it stolen?

What do you want for it?

It's not for sale.
Are you saying *this* spider could give someone Spider-Man powers?
Seriously, where did you get it?

No.
Osborn was *never* able to duplicate the process.
The Oz formula was a *complete* failure.
You can read about *that* online.

It's not a secret, Betty.
S.H.I.E.L.D. raided the laboratories.
Maybe the spider got loose during the chaos.

Wait, hold on...
Could *this* spider have given that *new* Spider-Man spider-powers?
Did the process work after all?

Hey!! Come back here!!
Oh, you *complete* nightmare!!
User!!

Oh please, that movie was the *worst.*
It was a masterpiece.
When you're older you'll see that--
What??
I'll pay you two to stop.
How much?
Brooklyn, New York.

Gotcha.
Well, I just became a very rich woman.

You don't say.

I know who the new Spider-Man is.
I have physical evidence.
I have proof.
It's a great story.
And I want you and I, right now, to work out our financial differences.
We have financial differences?
I don't like how much I make.
I don't like that I'm treated like a lesser reporter because of past indiscretions.

And I would like to rectify all of this in exchange for this world-wide exclusive.

Let me see it.

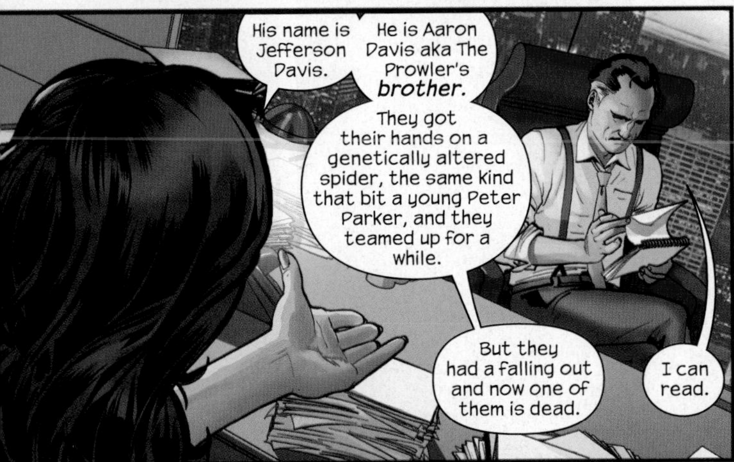

His name is Jefferson Davis.
He is Aaron Davis aka The Prowler's *brother.*
They got their hands on a genetically altered spider, the same kind that bit a young Peter Parker, and they teamed up for a while.
But they had a falling out and now one of them is dead.
I can read.

I'm not going to run this.

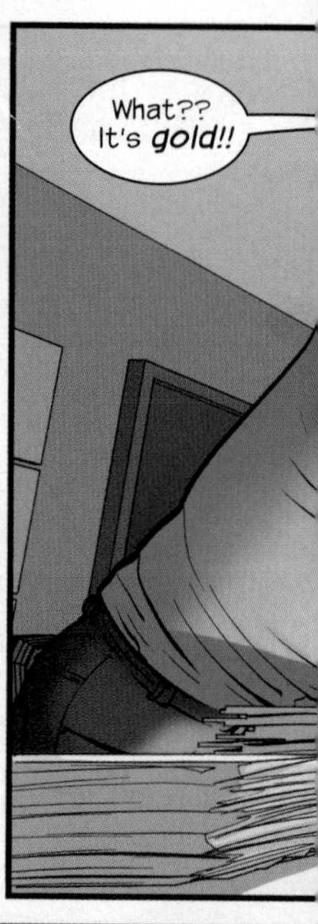
What?? It's *gold!!*

Okay, the world finds out this man is Spider-Man, which by the way, based on your prior record I'm not convinced is true...
You put that out there...*then* what?

Then the city has one less hero and this family's life is ruined.
The world will not be better.
Justice will not have been done.
You're just burying someone so you can...your words: make money.

You're *not* going to run this story?
No.
Well then I will *find* someone who will.
I'm sure you will.

You're *out* of your mind.

It's not a story.
Words *mean* something, Brant.
It's-- what?
Then what *is* it??
These words you're writing don't illuminate the truth.
They just-- all you're going to do is *ruin* a man.
Ruin his family.

I don't even know what you're *talking* about.

Everything that you've been through in your life, everything this city has been through... and you learned *nothing?*
That makes you a fool.

One of us will sleep very well tonight.

You bet!!
How much do you think I could get?

Really? No, I-I got it.
I got the *actual* spider that gave him his powers. I have it *in* my possession.
I have it on me *now.*

This is a *huge* relief. This is *great* news.
Ned Leeds told me what an amazing job you did getting him his book deal.
I should've done this *years* ago.

Really? *Letterman??*
If you can make *that* happen I will *marry* you!
Ha! Okay, great.
You got my number.
Thank you *so* much.

And you can officially suck it, you Hitler mustache-wearing--
Trying to profit off of things that don't belong to you.

Oh my God!!

Please, whatever it is that you--
CHUCK
Ggkk!

YOU really shouldn't do that.

VENOM WAR
19

Yiy!
This is hard.
I thought swinging around the city was going to be easy.
Did I just yiy?
I've never yiy'ed in my life!
Man, this webbing.
You have to think, what? Like five moves ahead.
You have to swing wide and hope that when you get to the end of your swing that there's something nearby you can web onto before you just kinda, well, fall.
Peter Parker made it look so easy.
It's fun. Yeah, sure.
THWAASSSSS
But it ain't--uh...

And...
I am out of webs.
Maybe no one noticed.
No. They noticed.
'Sup?
Stop watching me.
Stop watching me.
Stop watching me.
Stop watching me.
15:05
Embarrassing.

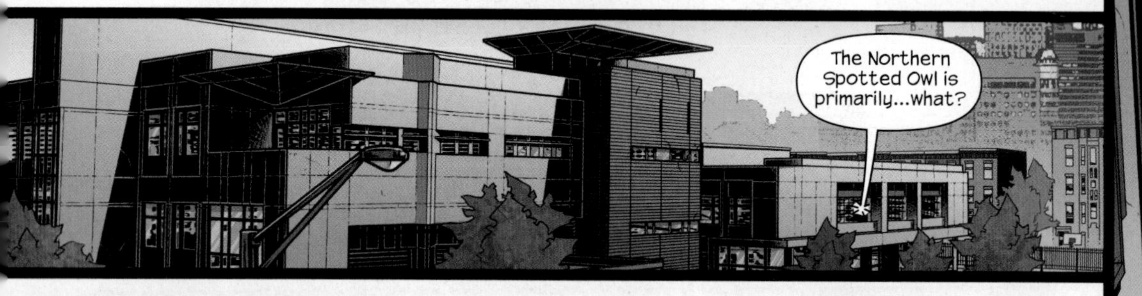
The Northern Spotted Owl is primarily...what?

Wood rats and flying squirrels. Yes, it's true.
EXCLUSIVE
SPIDER-SPAZ?
PLAY VIDEO ›

I'M TOTALLY OUT.

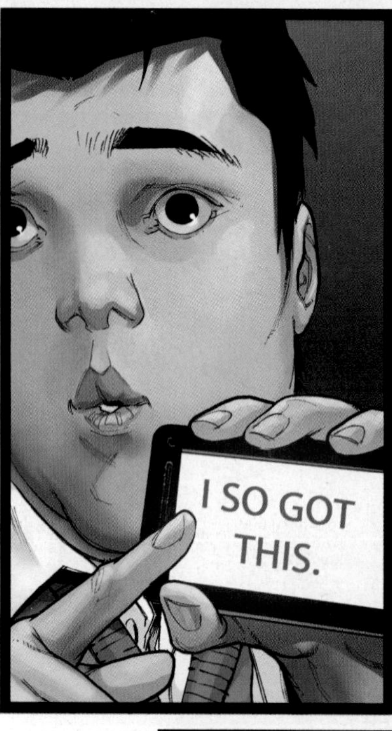
I SO GOT THIS.

Give it up, Ganke.
What?
The phone.
What phone?
I SO GOT THIS.

Ganke.
Ganke?
Yes.

Anyone?
Nocturnal.
That's right.
Its diet consists mainly of... what?
Insects.
Like maybe reptiles, birds, hmm?
I GOT IT.
Ganke?
Ganke.
Oh, you mean *this* phone.
It's not on.

SMASH

SMASH
BOOM

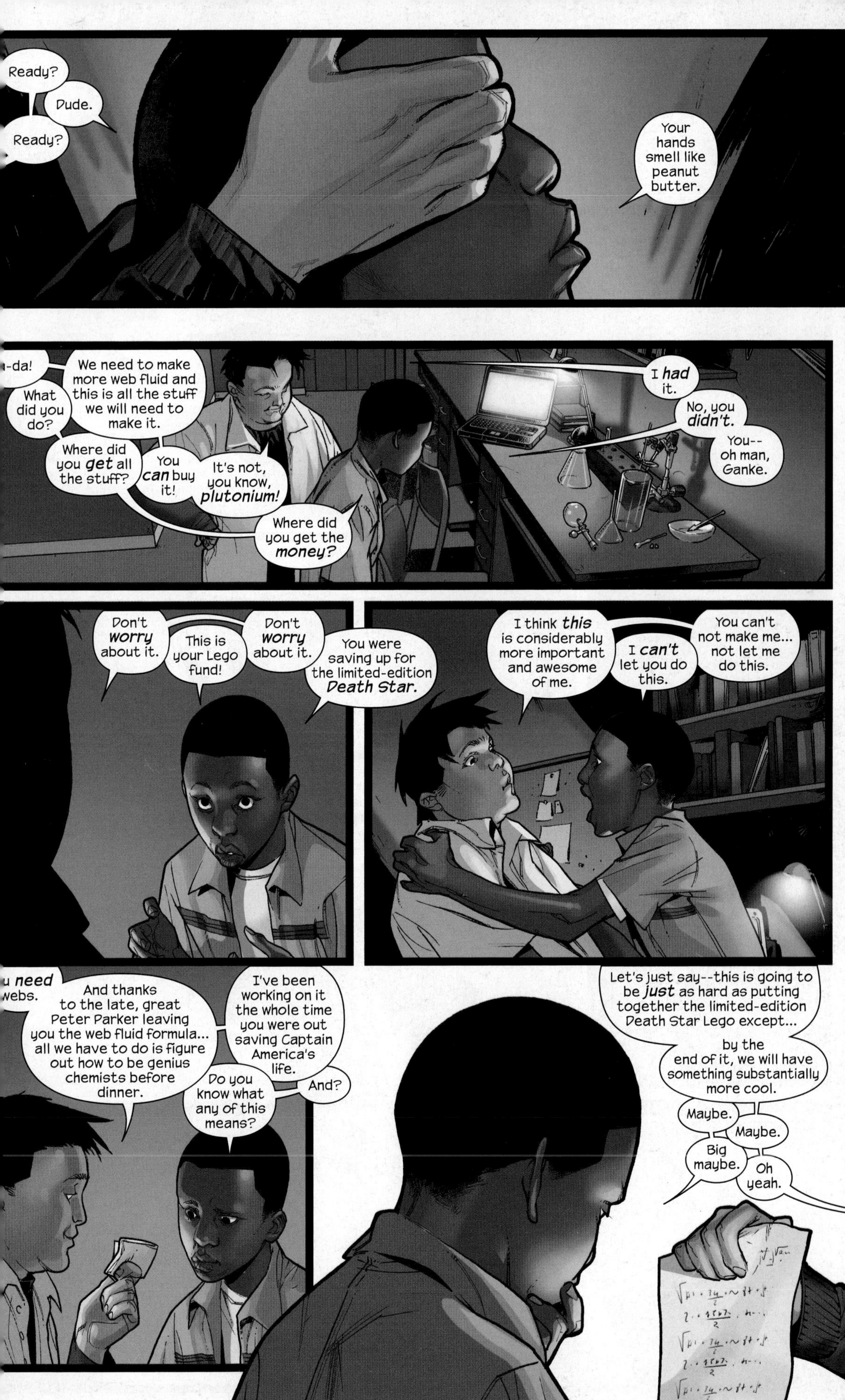
Ready?
Dude.
Ready?
Your hands smell like peanut butter.
-da!
We need to make more web fluid and this is all the stuff we will need to make it.
What did you do?
Where did you get all the stuff?
You can buy it!
It's not, you know, plutonium!
Where did you get the money?
I had it.
No, you didn't.
You-- oh man, Ganke.
Don't worry about it.
This is your Lego fund!
Don't worry about it.
You were saving up for the limited-edition Death Star.
I think this is considerably more important and awesome of me.
I can't let you do this.
You can't not make me... not let me do this.
u need webs.
And thanks to the late, great Peter Parker leaving you the web fluid formula... all we have to do is figure out how to be genius chemists before dinner.
I've been working on it the whole time you were out saving Captain America's life.
Do you know what any of this means?
And?
Let's just say--this is going to be just as hard as putting together the limited-edition Death Star Lego except...
by the end of it, we will have something substantially more cool.
Maybe.
Maybe.
Big maybe.
Oh yeah.

DAILY BUGLE.com

What can I do for you...?

Detective...?

Detective Maria Hill.

Homicide.

This is about Betty Brant.

Yes, it is, Mr. Jameson.

Yes, it is.

Well, obviously, I will help you in any way I can.

Jonah, I think you should wait for your lawyer to get here.

I'm not *guilty* of anything, Robbie.

Guilty people need their lawyers present.

The woman is dead. I wil help in any wa I can.

And so wi you.

She came to see you a couple of hours before the time of death...

Yes.

She was here about this time yesterday.

I'm sure my secretary has a log.

Do you remember what the conversation was about?

It wasn't pleasant.

Could you be more specific?

Wow.
Jonah, could I talk to you outside for a second...
obbie, I'm not oing to lie to the police.
As I'm sure you are aware, detective, she worked here for many years but last year I had to let her go because of what I considered to be unprofessional behavior.
She had a tendency to fraternize with people she was supposed to be reporting on.
Kraven the Hunter.
Kraven the Hunter was one of them. Yes.
She liked to be in the tabloids.
And making yourself the news story is not what a news person does.
Not on my paper.
And do ou know anyone ho would vant to ill her?
ad she been hreatened?
I really don't know that much about her.
Truthfully, she was a careerist, which means that everything she said to me by definition was her trying to advance herself.
I don't have much patience for that kind of person.
I told her a thousand times: You want to impress me?
Write well.
Did she tell you who this new Spider-Man was?

No.
She wanted me to pay her a great deal of money for that information.
She wanted her full-time job back and a byline.
I rejected the offer.
Because I don't care who the new Spider-Man is.
Why would you do that?
It's... news.
Maybe.
But it's not news I'm interested in reporting.
DAILY BUGLE
OBAMA WI ELECTION
Oh, oh, oh...I get it.
Because you knew Peter Parker...
Because I learned a lot from Peter Parker.
I learned a hero should be left to be a hero.
I publish a story saying who the new Spider-Man is, yes, I will sell a lot of papers.
But then this new Spider-Man would have to stop being Spider-Man.

And all of the good things he would do, whatever they would be, would never happen.
But someone *is* going to report the story.
She was going to sell it to ***someone.***
Except someone got to her before she could.
Yes.
That's true, isn't it?

Um, yes, our phone record showed that she was going to sell t story to a book publisher.
So I need to talk to a Ned Leeds.
Ned?
Is he a reporter here?
Yes.
Supposedly he had set her up with a potential publishing deal.
Well, that is disappointing to hear.
Okay, just, I'm sorry...
If you *know* she was going to walk out of here and sell the story because everyone else in your line of work will line up to *buy* the story...
why wouldn't you just publish it yourself?
Because it took almost a year after Peter Parker's death, but I just started sleeping well again.
I would like to continue doing that.
I'm, yeah, I'm going to have to take a look at her work computer.
Robbie will help you in any way, shape or form.
Robbie...

Miles' Parents' Apartment. Brooklyn, NY.
Slow down, Miles!
Hungry.
Do they not feed you at that school??
Yesshh!
Slow down. It's not a race.
BBZZZ

Who is it?
Work.
BBZZZ

You're not going to get it?
No.

KNOCK KNOCK
KNOCK KNOCK

Who is here?
I have it.
Please, Mr. Davis, we just want to get your side of the story...
Damn it.

Mr. Davis, Amy Lafuente, MSX News.
Can you confirm that it *was* you on the amateur footage that we have been running?
Was it you who faced off against the Hydra militia and saved the lives of a handful of New York civilians?
Can you tell us how you came to be in that situation??
He did *what?*
Oh no.
REC
How *dare* you??
You come to my work and you almost get me *fired!!*
I told you to *go away!!*
I told you I don't want to be part of *the circus!!*
I *told* you!!
But--but you're a *hero!!*
People want to *know!!*
Get out of my house!!
What the hey?
I'm going to *call the police.* You are *actually trespassing!!*
OUT!!
What you did was--
Agh!
Hey!
SLAM

Ow! My back!!
You're on a kid!
Yeah, uh, could you get off me, please!?

Why didn't you tell me this was happening?
24-hour news cycle.
It's a 24-hour news cycle.
It'll go away in 24 hours.
Why won't you talk to them and be done with it?

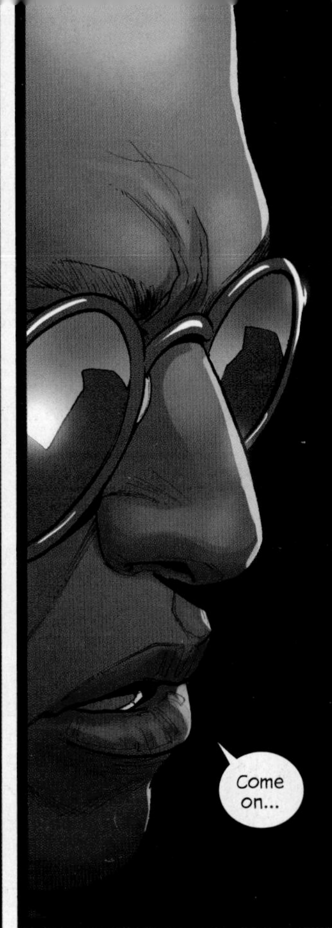

Come on...

Wait, what did you do?
I'm sorry, boy.
Sorry you had to see that.
You fought HYDRA??!!

I did too.
We--we have that in common.
Kind of.

Did you get that?
Wasn't much.
It was enough.

I--yeah, I know this--this was...weird.
Uh, yeah!!
Hydra??!! Dad??!!

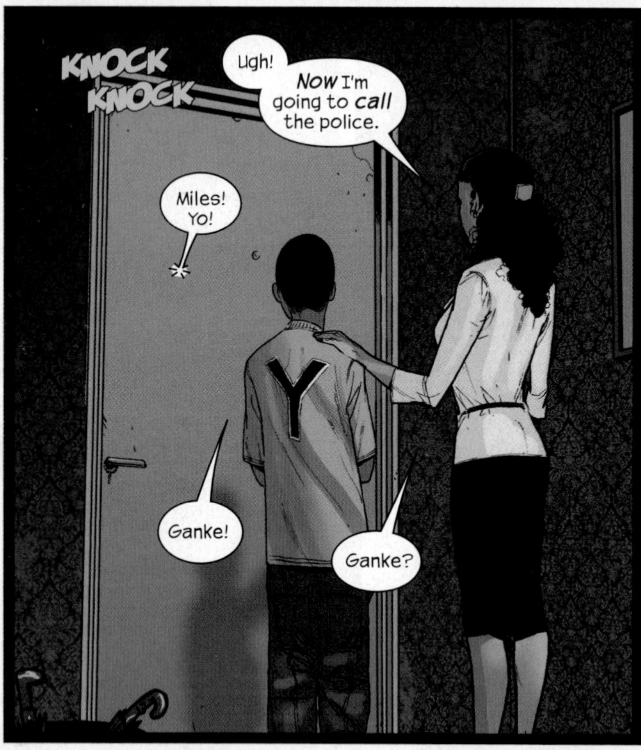
KNOCK KNOCK
Ugh! Now I'm going to call the police.
Miles! Yo!
Ganke!
Ganke?

Let me in.
Are they still out there?
No.

SLAM
Jefferson?

And he won?
Listen, he's upset.
Your dad doesn't like to fight.
Because it, you know, reminds him of who he used to be, and all that.
He doesn't want to fight anyone.
But he fought bad guys.
That's--that's insanely awesome.
I don't think it--I don't think it feels that way to him.
Wow.
anke, now's not a good me to--come right in.
They--did u see that? ey trampled me.
What's going on?
You will not believe this.
Jefferson?
Where are you going?
I'll be right back.
I just need some air.
Jefferson!!!

Hey man, all we needed was 14 seconds of B roll for the 11 o'clock and if that's the 14 seconds--
Uh-oh. Hey, he's here.
Oh, hey, change your mind?

All we want to do is get you on record. Tell your story.
Who told you where I live?
I looked it up--we, yeah, we looked it up.
I'm *unlisted*. As in: *not listed!*
Who told you where I live??

Buddy, listen, we're trying to--all we are trying to do is run a piece about a local man who rose up and acted like a hero.
Why are *you* acting like I just caught you stealing a handful of Slim Jims at the--

Who told you *where I live??!!*

I don't think I appreciate your--*holy!*
Oh my god!
What the...?
SSSSSS

RAWR

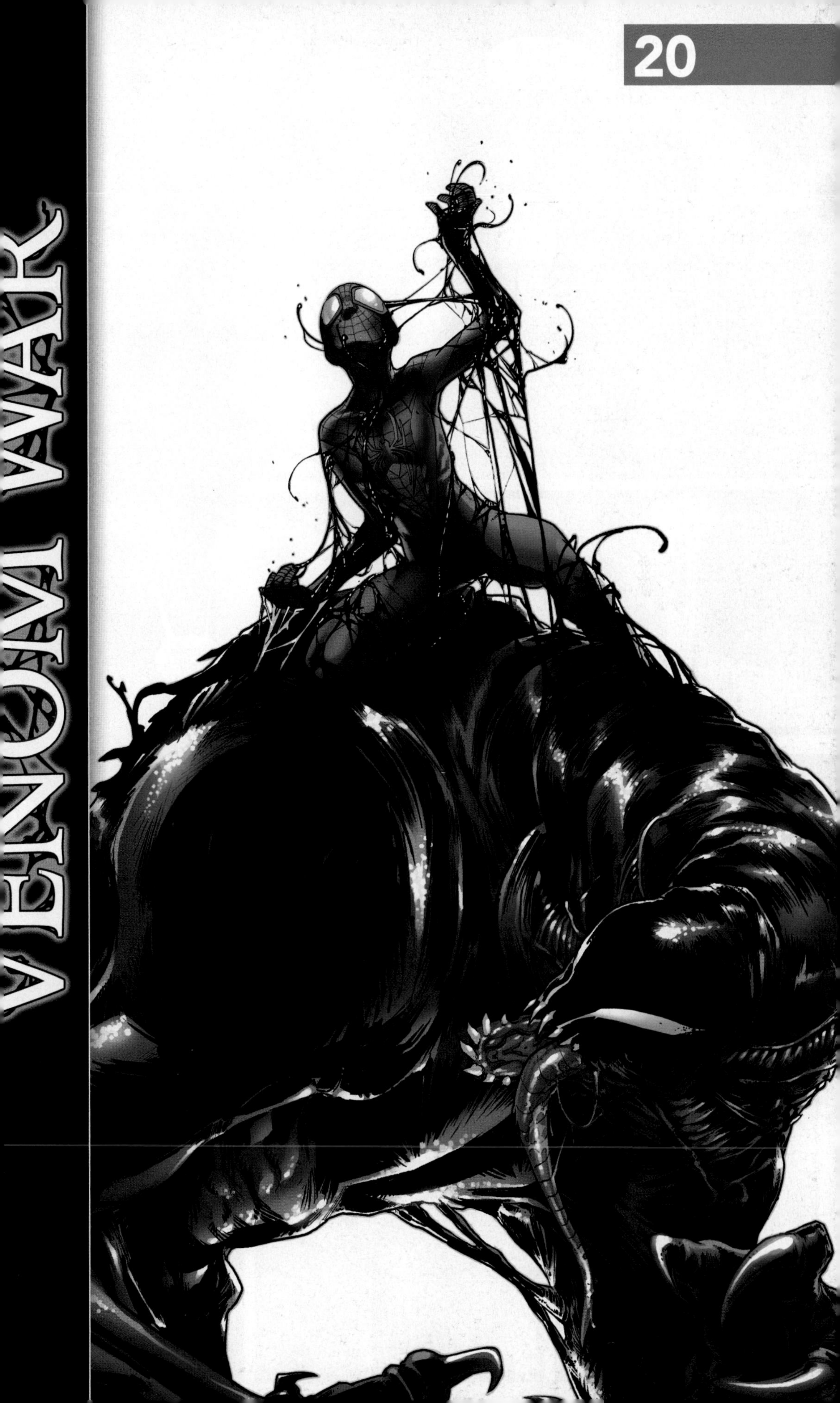

20

Mom? What's going on?

I'll--I'll be right back, Miles.

I'll come too.

You *stay* here.

Mom?

No, Miles.

You--you stay here and-and *do your homework.*

Ganke, go home.

Your family is going *crazy.*

My dad fought Hydra?

And he won?

Crazy.

I just said that.

AAAIIEEEEAA

CRA

Jefferson Davis.
The Spider-Man.
The brand-new Spider-Man.
Wh- what is--
Oh God, what is this?
Holy!

Oh!!
What is that?
Whoa!!
Your dad-he's--
Being attacked by a monster??!!
What is that?
Talk later!! Go!
Throw your mask on and go!!
Do you even know who I am??
I wonder.
Here, hey, wait, I did it.
This is why I came over.
I have more web fluid for you!!
Call the police!!
What is that monster thing? It looks familiar!
I'm calling The Hulk!

This is nuts!
Answer me, Jefferson!!
Do you know who I am??
Wh-wh-wh-what?
You're the best.
Go!
I'm the angel of death!

I *know* this thing!
SMACK

Gragghh!!

Uh, sir, you must get up out of the street!!

What voice am I doing?

An *English accent??* Idiot!

He's going to figure out I'm his son.

He's going to see right through this.

He's not stupid.

What--what is that? What is *happening?!*

Just *go!!*

Tell me you're getting this!

I just peed.

Oh my dear lord.

it, this--I know
ere I saw this!!

Peter Parker fought this thing!

I'm confused.

You're confused?

How did it end up here in front of *my* house??

Ok, so Spider-Man *isn't* who I thought he was!

You *are* much shorter in person...

Let's see who *you* really are.

Wait, what?

He thought *who* was Spider-Man?

Haarrghh!!
He thought my dad was Spider-Man?
What is this thing to even get that close to figuring out anything??
That's-- this is not good.
OFF DUTY
SMASSH
Hold on, focus!
I remember where I saw this--I saw it on YouTube!
Come here, little Spider-Man.
I'm dying to meet you. I've come such a long way.
The whole fight.
FUMP
REC
I have to remember what Peter did to-- AGH!!
WHACK

Heck with it. Just shut him down.

SHPACK
Arghh!

This...
...this also looked more impressive on TV.
DRIP

Oops.

Ganke.

Now you re desperately annoying me!!!

I came here for a reason and I'm not leaving until I do what I came here to do!!

Now all I have to do is figure out how to stop this before he blurts out my name, kills my family, or kills me!!

Ow!
Seriously, agh, all you people get out of this--this bloody place!
"Bloody place"--moron.
Do you people not speak English?!
GET OUT OF HERE!!
Think!!
How did Peter Parker school this guy??
All right, all right, all right, you.
First of all, yes, we haven't had proper introductions...
Whoa, hey, do you know this thing??
Is this related to what happened with you and Hydra?
Jefferson...
Oh my God!! What are you doing??!!
WHACK
Agff!!
Jefferson... no...
Think!
Who are you, Spider-Man??
Agh!
It was that spider.

You really think you're a hero?
Go!!
Aagghh!!
Are you going to take off your mask or am I going to have to take it off for you??
I am Spider-Man, the new hotness.
And you are??
CRACK
Gaaskk!
The
pider with
e number.
Do you
now what
at number
means?
Do you know how many more there are?

SMAASSHH
Haarrghh!

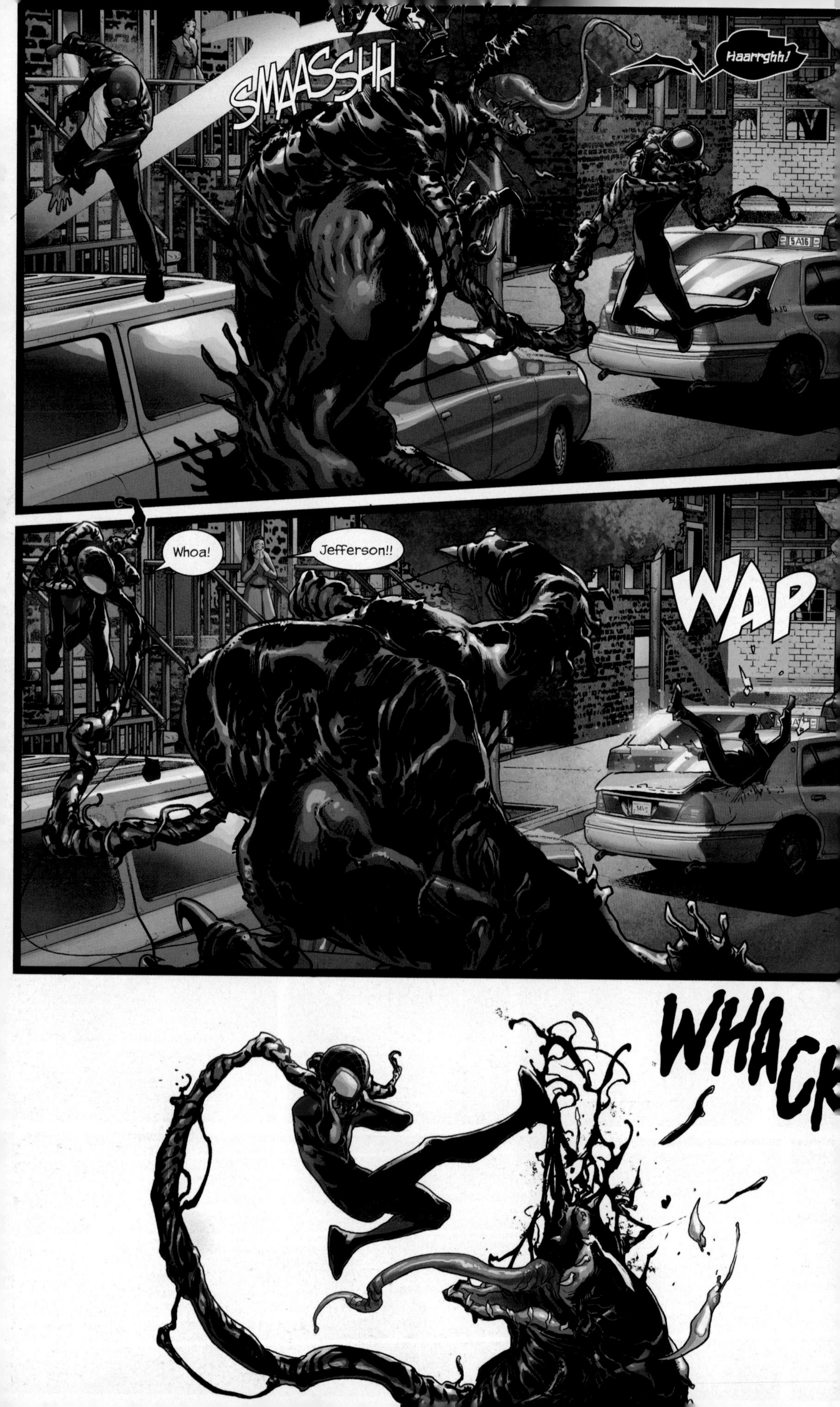

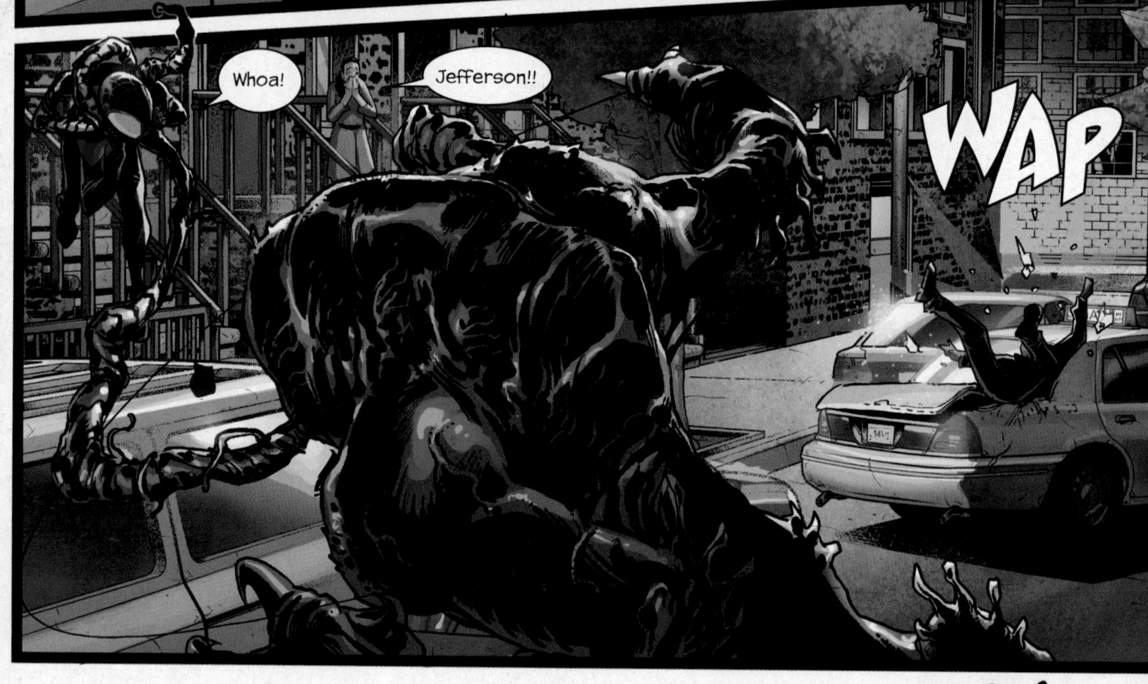
Whoa!
Jefferson!!
WAP

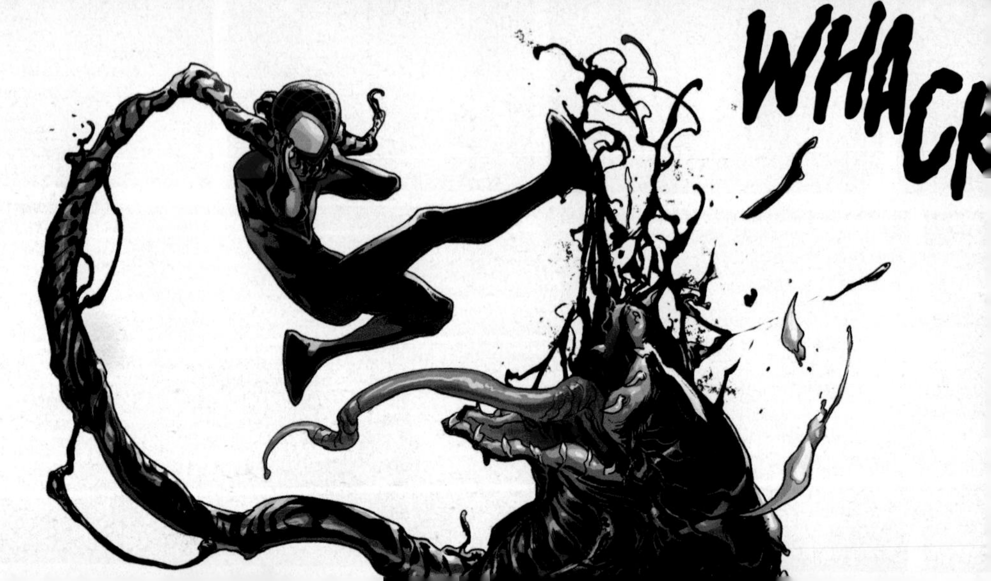
WHACK

AGH!
WHACK
I need, uhn, it's an emergency-- I n-n-need the police.
I need a-uh-an ambulance.
You're going to pay for that!!
SMASH

SMACK
Boom!
Hope that hurt!
Holy gazoongahs!
While I'm racking my brain trying to remember how Peter Parker beat this guy...
I just reminded myself that fighting super villains in front of his house is exactly how Peter Parker ended up dead.
I have to get this away from my house.
He knows about the spider.
CVARUMPLE
Agggee!!
Whatever this thing is, maybe it knows more about me than--AGH!
WEEEEOOOOOOOOOOWWWWEEOOOOOOOO
Holy!!
Police!!
LIE ON THE GROUND WITH YOUR HANDS OVER YOUR HEAD!!
NYPD

He--he--he's nconscious!! is breathing is--
His breathing is--
Hey, uh, come on, Ms. Morales!
We have to get off the street!!
This is car 97! We have a 616!!
Both of you-- on the ground-- now!!
Both of who? I'm not with him!
Holy!!
No!!
BAM BAM BAM
You do not!!
SPACK
SPACK
Whoa!
SPACK
SPACK
Gaargh!
NYPD

No!

Okay, didn't see *that*--***OW!***

Okay, maybe it's time we tried a ttle Venom blast.
ZAAATTTT
I have to stop forgetting I can do that.

Got to get back and help my mom before--
Agh!

Ev-everybody freeze!!
DOWN ON THE GROUND!!
NYPD
We need backup!!
Dispatch, do you read??!!!
BAM BAM BAM BAM BAM BAM

BAM
BAM BAM
Shooting??!! Just wait a sec and see if my venom blast does anything.

Come here so I can--wait--
What--
What did you just--

NO!

Jeez--
Louise.
Oh no.
No, no no no...
He's pouring into the sewer, maybe...is he dead? What was that thing?
He's getting away.
On the ground.
He's getting away!! Help me get it out of the--
On the ground!!
Dad.
On the ground-- now!!

SPSSSHOOO
SPSSHOOO
You lost him!
I lost him!
I think I see him!
Do not fire!!
You are not firing at a civilian apartment building!!
I think I see him!!
I'm going to eed you to step away from the body, ma'am.
What's his name? Do you know his name?
He--he--his breathing--
Je-je-je-
Jefferson.
F.D.N.Y.
AMBULANCE
Jefferson!!
Can you hear me, Jefferson?!
Jefferson?!

Oh man.
Okay, patient unresponsive, breathing irregularly at a rate of 2/min--
Call Brooklyn medical and tell them we are on our way.
Pinpoint pupils.
SpO2 of 86% on 2L.
No. Nonono...

Are you related to him, ma'am?
His wife. I'm his wife.
You can ride along *with* us.
Get ALS rolling.
We should wait till we get to the hospital.
We might not have time.

Ganke, I told you to go home.
I--
Where's Miles?
I--you--you told him to stay in the house.
I'm right her mom.

Dad?

Severe, blunt head trauma.
Apenic oxygenation.
Dude, ETCO2 tells you nothing about oxygenation.
I don't like the way he fell.
Spider-Man slapped him?
We'll get the statemen on the way.
Do we really *need* another Spider-Man?
Go. Go home with Ganke.
Listen to my words.
I'm coming with you.
Mom, I--
You *listen!!*

Watch your step, ma'am.
F.D.
F.D. N.Y.
AMBULANCE
F.D. N.Y.
AMBULANCE
Whoa, hey...
It's-- it's my fault.

VENOM WAR

Brooklyn.
Uggghh!
May I help you?
Fi-nally!
I'll have the biggest hot chocolate that exists on the planet.
I don't care if you have to go back there and get a bucket full of--
Mary Jane Watson?
Hey, Gwen.
You work here?
Kinda.
Hey, a job is a job.
You look good.
How come you don't ever call me back?
Did you call?
Like, weeks ago but after you never called me back I kinda got the hint.
I've been busy.
Can we not do this here?
I really don't want to...
Are you mad at me?
Is it about Peter, because--?
Oh no.

IDER-MAN BROOKLYN MONSTER ATTACK

TURN ON THE SOUND!!
I don't know how.
Dave?
We have customers, Ms. Watson.

LOCAL HERO BEATEN IN FRONT OF FAMILY

Oh man, is that--?
That thing attacked him at his home?
That *is* him, isn't it?
You have *a line!!*

Ugh!!
That kid has *no idea* what he's doing.
I'm going to go *help* him.
Where are you going?

Hello?? Miss Watson??
I'm not paying you to stare off into space!!

You're barely paying me anyhow.

Wait up!!

What do we got?!
African-American male. Thirty-thirty five years old!!
Car accident?
Spider-Man.
Spider-Man did this??
Spider-Man was fighting some kind of monster and this guy got in the way!!
Jefferson??

Lord, I hate this city!!
Take him into room six.
We're going to need to check him for radiation and--
Radiation?
You said monster. Well, monsters don't grow on trees.
We have a protoco for this.

We do??
Get room six prepped and I want X-Rays five minutes ago!!
Spider-Man?
I thought he died!

orales Apartment.
ooklyn, NY.
etective Hill, good.
We need you over here.
Is Spider-Man still around?
No, ma'am.
That monstery goo thing he was fighting?
Oh no. He--it disappeared.
Is anyone in pursuit?
Ma'am?
ursuit. Where ou chase after the bad guys.
It didn't exactly go down the way you--
Eyewitnesses?
A bunch of us on the job and we rounded up the civies over there.
Miles?
POLICE LINE - DO NOT CROSS

I don't see how this could possibly be your fault, Miles.

You don't see how a big Spider-Man villain showing up at my front door and beating my dad into the hospital could possibly be my fault?

(Man, I can't stop shaking...)
How did whatever that was know to come here?

I don't know.

What is that thing anyhow?
Ganke, I don't know.
From just now?
Oh, hey, I found some YouTube footage of it, I think.

No. No. From the Peter Parker, uh, era.
It's not very clear. It's kind of dark....
...but that's kinda the same thing, yeah?
With great power comes great responsibility.
What?

It's what
eter Parker
sed to say.
It's *why* he
was Spider-
Man.
But a day
like this...I think
it's the reason I'm
not supposed to
be Spider-Man!
This
isn't your
fault.

Instead of fighting that--that thing--I should have grabbed my mom and dad and swung them away from here and *saved* them.
Instead, I got into a fight that I had *no idea* if I could win or lose and *my dad*--!!
If you would've ran away with your mom and dad that thing would've *chased* you.

How is *that* a better plan??
You got that thing away from your parents as best you--
I'm going to the hospital!

Your mom told you *not* to.
Ganke, I know you're trying to *help* but--
There's nothing you can do there.

Maybe there is.
Hey, come on...remember when my dad died?

Remember how much help we were?
All they do at the hospital is tell you to *stay out of the way.*
And that doesn't mean your dad's gonna *die*, I'm just saying that we've been here before... we *know* what happens.

The best thing you can do is find out what this was and why they did it and how they know who you are...
...and shut it *down* before it happens again.
How?
I think we can help.

But first let's all get off the street.
This isn't the kind of conversation you have in public.
Yeah, that too.
In front of the police.
Uh... what *is* this?
Wow. Okay.
Gwen Stacy and Mary Jane Watson...
This is my best friend, Ganke Lee.
Uh...
uh...
S'up.
What are you *doing* here?
We saw it on TV.
We came right over.
How can you help?
I know a thing or two about a thing or two.
Follow me.

NY
Gyyaaagghh!!!!
Hurraaaaaagghh!!!

Whoa!
What was that?
HURRAAAGH!
Hello?
What are you doing?
Someone is hurt down there.
Yeah... that doesn't sound like a person.
Ooaaagghh!!
Are you okay?
Dude! Are you insane? Let's go.
You need me to call someone?
Oh my God!!
Oh no!!
Ho! Hey!!
HELP!!
Aaggee!

Oh God!!
BEEP BOOP BOOP

911 emergency.

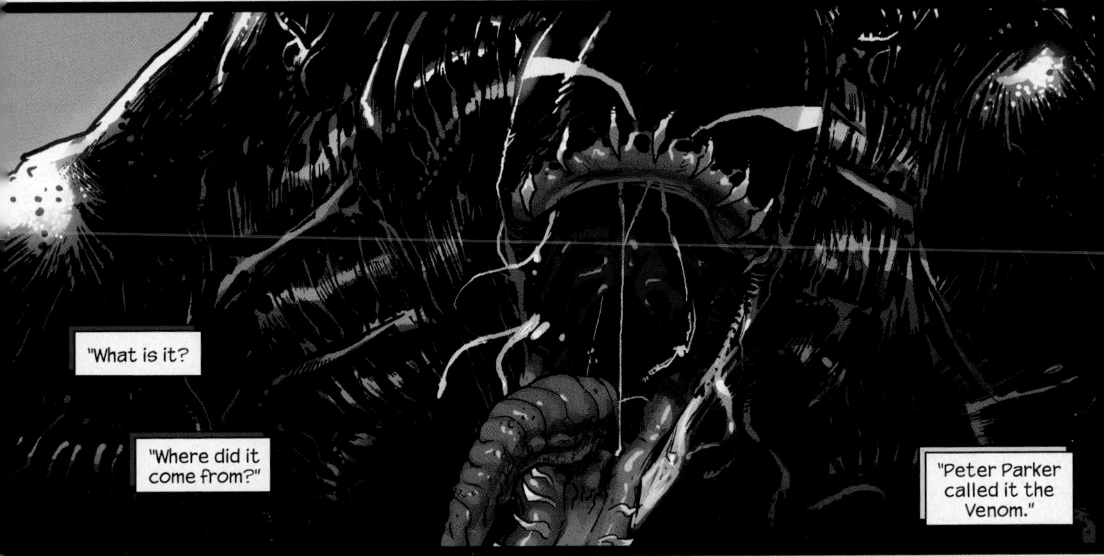

"What is it?
"Where did it come from?"
"Peter Parker called it the Venom."

Peter Parker's father was working on a cure for cancer and he accidentally created it.
What?
Wow.
Yes.

Peter Parker ha father

No.

That's what *that* thing is. It's a parasite.
It needs a host--a body to become what it is.
No host. No monster.
But with a host...
Well, you saw it.

Obviously it thinks this is where Spider-Man lives.
And obviously it's right.

My father is in the hospital.
Well, I think Venom maybe knows now that your father maybe *isn't Spider-Man*.

How do *you* know so much abou all this?

erybody
a father.
lied when
ter was
a kid.
And he
eated *that*
monster?

No.
He created a cure for cancer that *someone else* turned into this monster.
DAILY BUGLE
Research scientists among dead in plane cras
Peter's father would *never* let them use it for, like, the military or anything like that.
It *might* have been what got Peter's dad killed.
Do you know what a symbiote is?
Ever hear the word?

PUNK!!

Where did it come from and why was it here?

But he didn't attack *me.*
He attacked my father.

Maybe he thinks *your father* is Spider-Man.

You have to tell him...

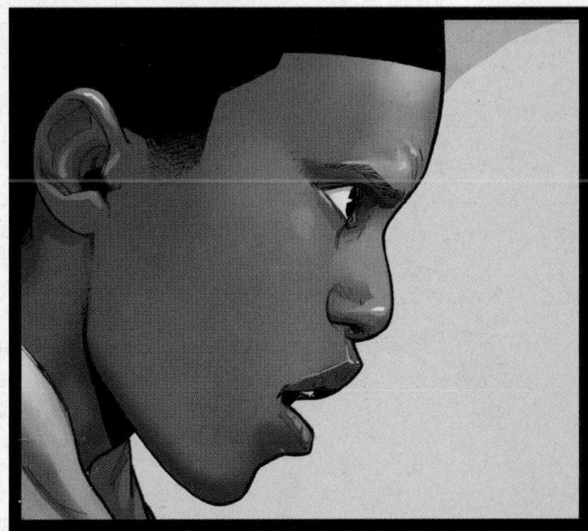

I used to be one.

I'm sorry, *what?*

I was killed by one of those.

You *died?*

But then, thanks to Peter, thanks to a lot of things...
I was separated from it.
The part of it that was me got to be me again.
And here I am.
Now, I don't remember much of what I'm telling you.
I'm just repeating what Peter Parker told me.

She *was* dead.
This is an insane miracle.
I got a second chance.
A lot of people who came in contact with this thing were not so lucky.
So I'm telling you...
This fight you had tonight, with this thing...
It could have gone a lot worse.

What does it want from me?
Forget that...what is death like?

Infinite nothingness.
I knew it.
This *Venom* has a deep-rooted DNA genetic connection to the Parker bloodline.
It was originally created from Peter's father's DNA.
It literally stalked and hunted Peter once he...it realized who Peter was.

Now with Peter gone, it may just be looking for *you* because, like him, *you* became Spider-Man.
So whatever was special about Peter Parker genetically... you might have the same thing.
You were bit by a spider too.

Yeah...
Just like Peter...
Yeah.
Peter was bit by a spider that was being genetically experimented on at--
Oscorp.
That's right.

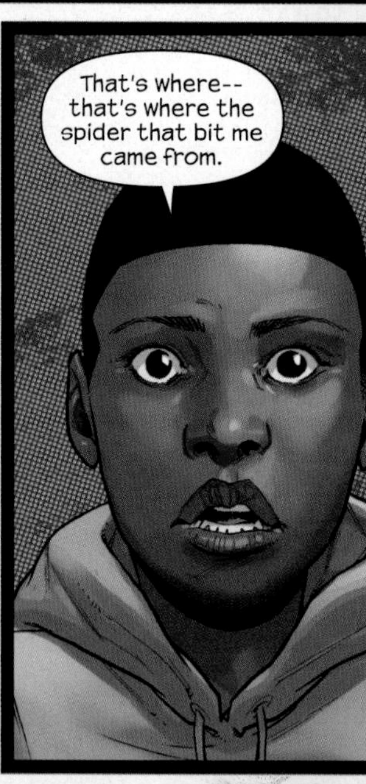
That's where--that's where the spider that bit me came from.

Now look at this!
This *just* happened. Like, yesterday.
Someone broke into the long abandoned Oscorp laboratories and *destroyed it.*
Blew it all up.
DAILY BUGLE
WIN A 50G FORTUNE TODAY!
Oscorp's main facility destroved

The exact same lab where Peter got bit by the spider.
She was there.
I know. I was there when he got bit.
You guys are freaking me out.
I'm having a good time.
Excuse me?

What is going on here exactly?
Wait, whoa, uh, you can't just come in here.
Get out of here before we call the--

I know you.

I am the detective working on your uncle's death case.
And now here I am again, Miles, because *your father* was attacked in *another Spider-Man* situation.
Wait, whoa, you can't just come in here.
You need a warrant. You need probable cause.

love when *Law and rder* has a marathon nd everyone thinks they know the--
Gwen Stacy. That's right.
Captain John Stacy was your dad.
My *dad* was a cop, genius.

Yeah.
My condolences. What happened to him I wouldn't wish on--
Yeah, great. You should leave.
I would but I can't help but wonder...

Peter Parker's ex-girlfriend and the girl who now lives in his house are here pow-wowing with *these* little boys all the way out here in *Brooklyn.*

Please--
please leave my house.

You're in a lot of trouble, young man.
This thing that you fought tonight...
Two days ago, a reporter from the Daily Bugle, the paper where Peter Parker used to work...
She says she found out who the new Spider-Man really is.

Except she was murdered in her home.
Violently.
Traces of this *goo monster* all over her house.

Your uncle is dead, your father is in intensive care and murdering monsters are showing up on your front door.
Whatever you and your little pals here are up to, whatever you know...
I can't help you unless you let me.

Anything you want to share with me before someone *else* gets hurt... or worse?

S-someone was killed? For real?
We don't know what you're talking about and we don't have anything to say to you.
And my tablet takes great HD movies.
I'm making a movie right now of a police detective breaking and entering a private home and threatening minor children.

This isn't a game.
[REC]
People are being hurt.
People are dying.

That was nuts.
She's the police!
Kid, you were going to tell her what we know?
She could be the Venom for all we know.
Oh, yeah.

You all right, kid?

"What are you going to do?"

Rio Morales?
Me!!
Me. That's me.

Come with me, please.
Is he okay?
The doctor will talk to you about--
Just tell me if he is okay!
Ma'am, I-- it's not my place.

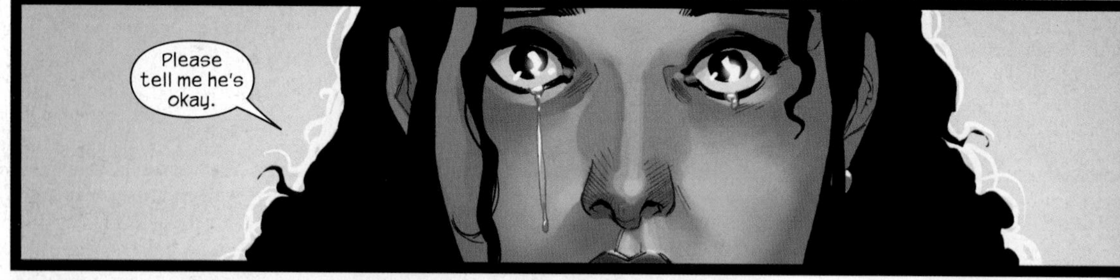
Please tell me he's okay.

Aagghh!!
Holy!!
What the @#$@$@!!??

22
VENOM WAR

Morales Apartment.
Brooklyn, New York.

Dude, that cop totally knows you're Spider-Man.
What are you going to do?

You can't let her think you're Spider-Man.
She already thinks it, Gwen. There's not much he can do.
He didn't deny it, MJ. He just stared at her.

This was the mistake Peter Parker made.
Too many people ended up knowing who he was.
Too many people knew and eventually the wrong person finds out.
Who knows what kind of person she is?

What are you going to do?

Hey!!
You, lady!
Is there something you want to tell me?
You're wrong.
I'm not who you think I am.
Then I'm wrong.
Except I'm not.

There is a monster killing people out on the street!!
And--and--and you walk into my house and accuse me--
You want me to what? To prove it?
I'm a police detective and I used to be an agent of S.H.I.E.L.D.!
How long you think it will take me to frisk you and find your mask?

You--you can't just...
I know you're hurting. I know you're upset.
I know you don't know what's going on here so let me give you some advice--
We gotta 616!!

We have 616!! 616 at Brooklyn General!!
What is it??
NYPD
That thing--that thing that was here went there!!
That thing is tearing up the hospital right now!!
They called it in!!
All units.

Is that--is that where they took my father?
You'll get there faster than we will.

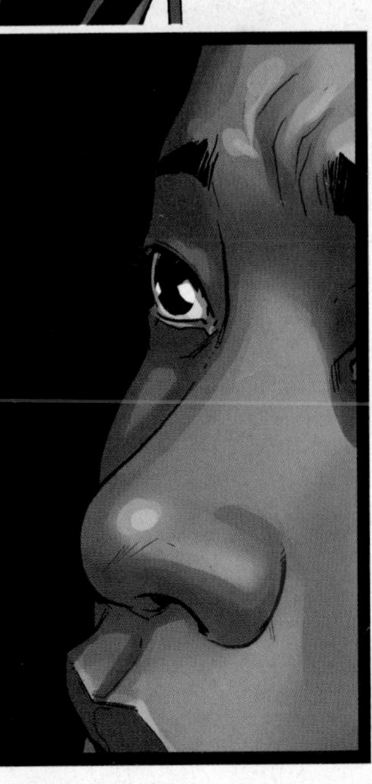

Kid!
Listen to me, don't fight him head-on!!
You grab as many civilians and sick people as you can and you get the hell away from that thing.
I'll call S.H.I.E.L.D.!! I'll get the Ultimates!!
GO!!
What's happening??
Oh my God!

-rooklyn General.
Where is he??!!
Where is my beloved Spider-Man?!

I've got you!
What is happening??!! Is it terrorists??

His name is Jefferson!! Where is he?!
Ggkkss!!
Oh lordy!!

What is happening??
I don't know!!
Turn off the lights!!
Why's everyone yelling?? I don't like yelling!!

Where is my Spider-Man??!!
I will spare you all your pain just give me my Spider-Man!!

Spider-Man.

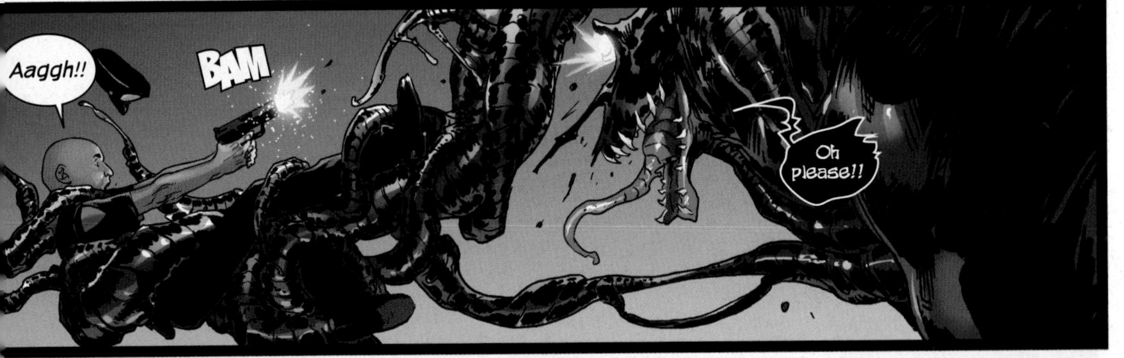
Aaggh!!
BAM
Oh please!!

This is what you want?!
This blood is on your hands!!
Agh!
Aiaafkk!
Take the patients!! Get them out of here!!
Where are the police?!

His name s Jefferson Davis!!
He's nothing to you!!
He's everything to me!! He's mine!!
Give him to me and I'll leave you to die in peace!!

He's-- that thing out there is talking about this man...
Call the police and turn off the light!!

Give me y Spider-Man d I'll give you your life!!
Give me my-!!

AAAAAARGGGHHHHHHHH!!

WHAM
ZZAATT

SMACK

I hit him with all of the Venom blast I have.
What does it take to knock this--??

ZZAATT

WHAM

ZZAATT

Come on, you coward!! Show me who you really are!! Show me--
SMACK

CRASH
Aghh!
Ow.

Ggsskk!

Now I understand!! I had the wrong one!! I didn't see that you were just a boy!!
Gskk!

you'll have to forgive me. I haven't been thinking clearly...

BAM
BAM
BAM
I haven't been myself! I'm not right. But I think that's about to--
Nyaaagghh!!

BAM BAM BAM
Get your hands off him!!

Mom!
CRASH

Get out of here!!
Are you crazy?? Get out!!

Get out of here beforRRMMM!!

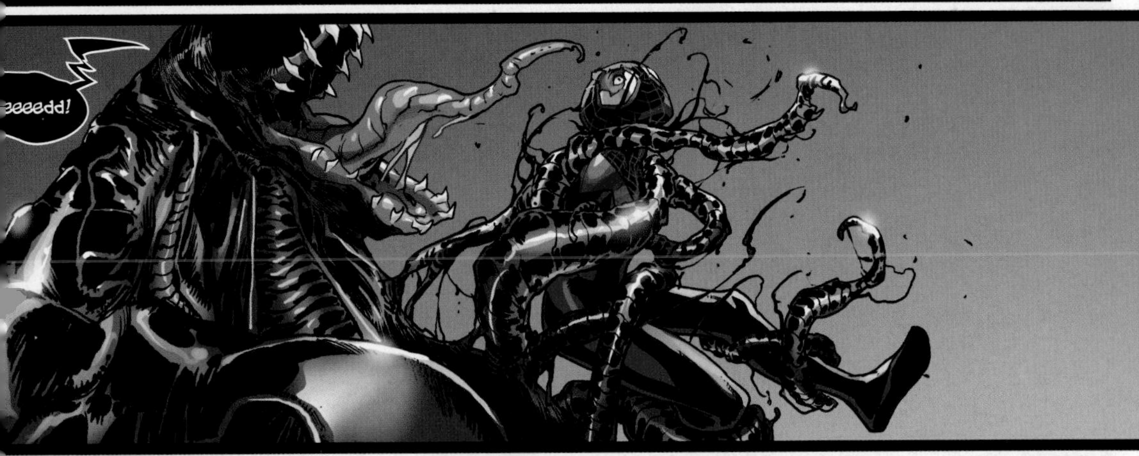
eeeedd!

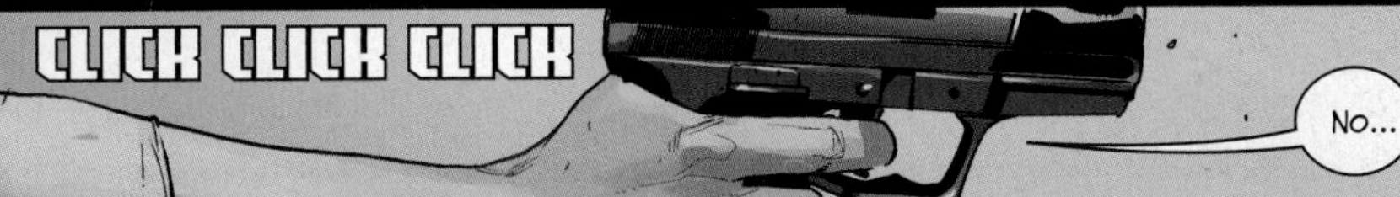
CLICK CLICK CLICK
No...

I know now!
The answer to all my future is inside you.
Neeeed it.
Yyeessssss!!
NNOOO!

And what to do with you?
Please, I beg you...
I'll do whatever you want...
Please give me back my son.
Your son?
Your family has caused me a lot of trouble!!
You have no idea what I have done to get to--
What I--
No!

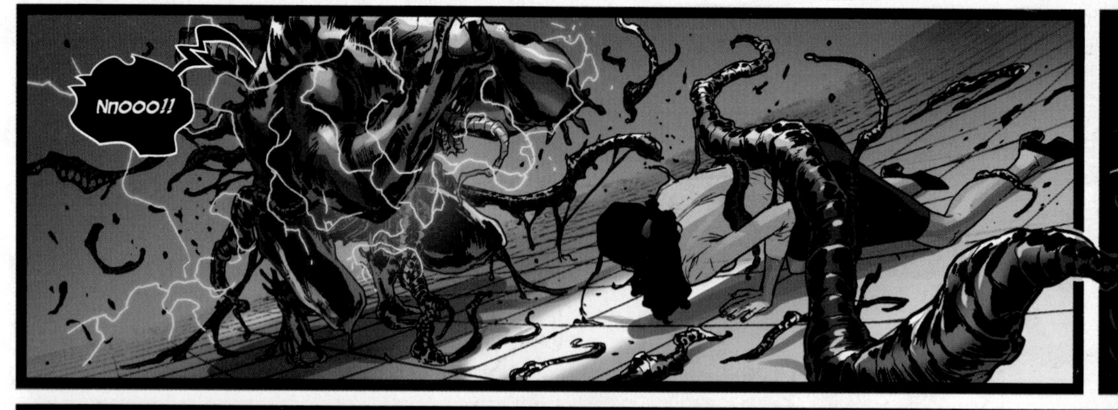
Nnooo!!

Naaarrrgghh!!

BAMBAMBAMBAMBAMBAMBAMBAM
Police!!
DOWN NOW!!

Aaaiiee

New York PD!!
If you can hear my voice, evacuate this building immediately!!

Nntaaagghh!!
BAMBAMBAMBAMBAMBAMBAM
BAMBAMBAM
Who is this guy?

I have no idea.

What the--
BAMBAMBAMBAMBAMBAMBAMBAMBAMBAMBAMBA
SPLAT
SPLAT
SPLAT

Come on, let's get out of--

A doctor!! *I need a doctor!!*
ok at ou.
Look what you can do.
Baby, don't ever let him know.
Don't ever let your father--
Oh no.

We need to evacuate the entire hospital.
This is a lethal chemical hazard, people.
Everyone get away from anything that looks like--
Come on, this way!
How do you know?
Because everyone is running the other way.
No!!
You're going the wrong way!!
You need to get out of this hospital immediately!!

His name is Dr. Conrad Marcus.
Reports are already coming in that this divorced doctor of biochemistry is, or I should say was, on staff at the research and development division of the Roxxon Corporation.
We are still waiting for official word from Roxxon as to what they know about this man and how this has all come to pass...
ROXXON industries
Was Marcus' violent mutation some sort of experiment or accident gone wrong?
Police have yet to officially confirm that Marcus is responsible for the numerous deaths associated with this "Venom monster."

You will inform the media that the Roxxon Corporation is working with authorities in all capacities so that this terrible tragedy can be put behind us.
Mr. Roxxon, a--are we working with-- I mean--
With police?
Police are downplaying reports that this new Spider-Man personally knew...

What we are doing is making sure that no one can connect what happened tonight to what's happening here.

What we are doing is waiting until this all blows over and then we will find out exactly what this @#$@# Marcus was doing with the symbiote in the first place.

What we are going to do is wait until no one is watching us... and when I give the word I want to find out how Spider-Man ***became*** Spider-Man and why ***we can't figure out how to make a Spider-Man for ourselves!!***

Spider-Man.

Mm.

No more!
NO MORE!!
NO MORE!!

No more!!
No more!!
The End.